How to Write a 5th Grade (or any other grade) Essay

by Kathleen Powers, M.S. Ed.

D1304294

How to Write a 5th Grade
(or any other grade) Essay
by Kathleen Powers, M.S. Ed.

ISBN 978-0-692-06460-3

Table of Contents

Figure 1. Illustration by Anne Trombetta
(www.annetrombetta.com).

About the Author

Kathleen Powers is a private tutor of writing for students in pre-K through high school. She has worked as a newspaper reporter and editor and as a teacher in middle grades, high school and college. She writes two blogs. Comicphonics.com advises adults how to teach reading to little children. EnglishWritingTeacher.com advises how to write better and how to teach writing to children. Mrs. Powers lives in the north Atlanta suburbs.

Acknowledgements

One hundred thousand thank yous Bill, for encouraging me to write the blog, EnglishWritingTeacher.com, from which so much of this book comes. Thank you too for suggesting I turn the blogs into a book for students. Thank you for doing the computer work to start the blog and keep it going. Thank you, especially, for all your work on this book--creating the cover design, charts and graphs and for tedious hours of formatting. You are wonderful!

Thank you, Anne, for launching comicphonics.com with me and for making EnglishWritingTeacher.com more attractive with your illustrations and your good ideas. And especially, thank you for your year-in, year-out support. We make a good team.

Thank you, too, to all my students for teaching me to become a better writing teacher. Especially, thank you Amber, Andrew, Grace, Hannah, Mahika, Nilan, and Ryan for allowing me to share a bit of your work here.

✗

Introduction

An essay is writing that starts with an introduction, including a main idea / thesis. The body supplies back-up details to support that main idea. An essay ends with a conclusion. An essay focuses on one main idea and two or more supporting ideas, all backed by details, lots and lots of details.

In this book,

- you'll learn how to narrow a topic.

- you'll learn how to choose and use a prewriting organizer.

- you'll learn how to write different kinds of introductions and conclusions.

- you'll learn how to transition.

- you'll learn how to revise, to read your words aloud, to strengthen verbs, to vary sentence openings and lengths, to add details, to combine sentences, and to eliminate sentences.

Most lessons are a page long. Some are illustrated with the work of real students your age. If those students can do it, so can you.

K. Powers

P.S. An essay is like a recipe: You need certain ingredients and you need to add them in a particular order. This book teaches you how.

1.0 Choose a topic

1.1 Narrow your topic

You might think you need to choose a big topic like video games to write enough information for an essay. Wrong. Choosing a smaller topic is better.

How can you narrow your topic? If your topic is the American Revolution, for example, list subtopics such as people, battles, acts of Parliament, Tories, boycotts, the Declaration of Independence, and Valley Forge. But these subtopics are too big.

Take one of the subtopics—say the battles—and choose one battle, such as Lexington and Concord. Now divide Lexington and Concord into subtopics, such as British uniforms, the shot heard round the world, guerilla warfare, and Paul Revere's ride.

Still too big. Okay, take one of those subtopics and divide it into subtopics. Suppose you take Paul Revere's ride. The old North Church, Paul Revere's horses, rowing across the river, and Paul Revere's escape when was captured by soldiers are still too big to be good essay topics.

But you are narrowing your topic. What if you research the two lanterns in the tower of the old North Church? Who decided on two lanterns? Who lit them? What did one lantern mean? What did two lanterns mean? When did Paul Revere see them? Congratulations! You went from a huge topic to a small but much more interesting topic. It takes work to narrow down a good topic. See Figure 2.

Possible topics for Revolutionary War essay

Important people, battles, acts of Parliament, Tories, boycotts, the Declaration of Independence, smallpox and Valley Forge. Battles of Lexington and Concord, Battle of Bunker Hill, Battle of Trenton, Battle of Saratoga, and Battle of Yorktown. British uniforms, the shot heard round the world, guerilla warfare, and Paul Revere's ride. Who gave the signal for Paul Revere to go? The old North Church, where did Paul Revere get horses? Did he ride alone? How did he row across the river without the British noticing? How did he escape when he was captured? Two lanterns, who decided on two lanterns? Who lit them? What did one lantern mean? What did two lanterns mean? Where was Paul Revere when he saw them?

Figure 2. Narrowing a topic

2.0 Prewriting Organizers

2.1 Use a prewriting organizer

Do you think you can skip organizing your ideas before you write sentences? Or do you think scribbling three or four words is enough planning before you write? Think again. Your teachers can tell when you have not planned your essays. In unorganized essays,

- the ordering seems awkward;
- the details are too few, too general, or lopsided;
- the essay might not focus on one main idea.

Essays are not a string of text messages. Writing down ideas as they pop into your head does not create an organized essay. You must plan before you write, and your plan must be obvious to your reader.

Rubrics used to grade student essays usually give three-fifths of your final grade for developing a single idea and organizing that idea clearly. That's 60% of your grade for organizing and sticking to your plan. See Figure 3 on the next page.

Think of a prewriting organizer as Lego® instructions for a new spaceship. Could you ignore the instructions, put together the Lego® pieces any which-way, and end up with a spaceship?

Your essays—and your grades—will improve so much if you organize your essays first.

Typical Fifth Grade Rubric
for Writing Assessment

Ideas = 40%

Controlling idea well developed?	1 2 3 4 5
Controlling idea focused?	1 2 3 4 5
Controlling idea develops assigned topic?	1 2 3 4 5
Supporting ideas relevant and clear?	1 2 3 4 5
Enough information?	1 2 3 4 5
Complete ideas?	1 2 3 4 5
Ideas easy to understand?	1 2 3 4 5
Awareness of genre?	1 2 3 4 5

Organization = 20%

Organizational plan obvious?	1 2 3 4 5
Sequence clear?	1 2 3 4 5
Introduction and conclusion work?	1 2 3 4 5
Paragraphs well organized?	1 2 3 4 5
Transitions?	1 2 3 4 5

Style = 20%

Appropriate language?	1 2 3 4 5
Writer's voice apparent?	1 2 3 4 5
Literary language?	1 2 3 4 5
Advanced vocabulary?	1 2 3 4 5

Conventions = 20%

Sentence structure and punctuation?	1 2 3 4 5
Errors that interfere with meaning?	1 2 3 4 5

Figure 3. Developing and organizing ideas is 60% of a final grade.

2.2 List organizers

A list can be a prewriting organizer, but it's not a good one. A list has advantages and disadvantages.

Advantages:

- Writing a list is easy. You feel like you are making progress as your paper fills up.

- You don't need to organize your ideas before you begin.

- You can write almost anything on your list.

- Anyone can write a list. You need no training.

Disadvantages:

- When you write a list, you wind up with some good ideas and some bad ones.

- When the list is complete, you need to get rid of bad ideas and figure out what ideas go together.

- You can easily go off-topic with a list.

- You waste time thinking of useless ideas.

- What starts out quickly slows down as you later organize your ideas.

Here is a list by a third grader that still needs to be organized.

Topic: My three favorite dinosaurs

- brachiosaurus
- herbivore
- long neck to eat tree leaves
- theropods
- tyrannosaurus rex
- carnivore
- sauropods
- raptors
- archaeopteryx
- feathers plus wings
- paleontology
- fossils
- thousand-pound hearts
- claws for tearing prey
- eggs up to 11 pounds
- link between dinosaurs and birds
- earlier dinosaur
- later dinosaur
- swung neck side-to-side
- ran fast
- flew
- hardly moved at all

To organize this list, the student could label all the "brachiosaurus" items with the letter "B" or he could highlight those items in one color. He could select all the tyrannosaurus rex items and label them with a "T" or highlight them a different color. He could do the same for archaeopteryx items. Lastly, he could number the dinosaurs in the order he would write about them. So, after the quick list is done, the student still needs to organize his essay.

2.3 Table organizers

If you are comparing or contrasting two or three ideas, a table can be a good prewriting organizer.

Advantages:

- You can easily see similarities and differences.

- The categories are clear.

- Creating a table goes pretty fast.

- You can list categories in any order.

Disadvantages:

- When the table is filled, you still need to organize it. What categories should go together for one paragraph? What categories should you write about first, second, and third?

- You may wind up with one idea with lots of details and another idea with little information.

- You may need to go back to the table and add more categories if you see that your information is lopsided.

See Figure 4 on the next page for the same information we looked at in a list on the previous page. Notice how the table is more organized than the list.

Name	Brachiosaurus	Tyrannosaurus Rex	Archaeopteryx
Group	Sauropod	Theropod	Raptor
Food	herbivore	carnivore	carnivore
When	Middle Jurassic	late Cretaceous	late Cretaceous
Covering	scales	scales	feathers
Teeth	flat molars	serrated, conical	canines
Claws	no	yes, sharp	yes
Size	80,000 pounds	14,000 pounds	2-4 pounds
Features	huge heart, eggs	huge jaws, tiny arms	wings

Figure 4. A table organizer is good for comparing or contrasting ideas.

2.4 Mind web organizers

Do you skip using prewriting organizers because you think they are hard to make? Maybe what you don't like are the kinds of prewriting organizers that you use in school.

What I recommend for informational (expository) essays and persuasive (argumentative) essays is a mind web organizer, sometimes called a spider web. You write the single topic of the essay in the middle of the paper, and then, like spokes of a bicycle wheel, you draw two, three or four lines out from the center. At the ends of those lines, you write each subtopic you will develop. From each of those subtopics, you draw new "spokes" for the details you want to use.

After the details are added, it helps if you encircle each mind web subheading and all its details in a different color, using colored pencils, markers, or crayons. Why? Using color is a visual way to connect details that belong together. Also, you can see which subheadings have too few details and you can add more details before you write your first draft.

The last thing you need to do is number each group of ideas in the order in which you want to write about them in your essay.

Figure 5 on the next page was made by a third grader. This mind web organizer shows details which go together in different shades because this book is in black and white. When the student made it, he used colors. Each of the shaded sections is numbered to show the order the student wanted to use.

2.5 Why do mind webs work?

- With a single idea in the middle of the web, you remember to write about one idea only.

- With two, three, or four "spokes," you can create enough—but not too many—subtopics.

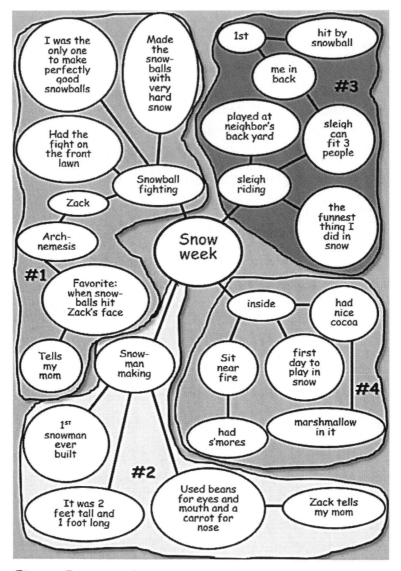

Figure 5. A mind web can be an easy way to develop and organize your ideas.

- The easy-going way of creating a mind web relaxes you. You think, "This isn't hard. I can do this."

- If you run out of room on your paper, you can turn the paper sideways or draw arrows to more information on the back. Or you can tape another paper to your mind web.

- Even after you begin your first draft, you can add details to your mind web.

The result is a detailed prewriting organizer about a single topic. Sometimes it looks messy, but the only ones who need to read it are you and maybe your teacher. Your parents might be shocked at how messy it looks, but later, when you show them the good essay you write, they will love mind webs.

Figure 6 on the next page takes the information in Figure 5 and turns it into an informational essay. Each paragraph is circled with the shade that corresponds to the four shaded sections of Figure 5.

2.6 Time line organizers

I recommend you use a modified time line to plan your narratives. Narratives tell stories, either fiction, such as a detective story, or nonfiction, such as the life of a butterfly. Those stories are clear if you write them in chronological (time) order.

When I say modified time line, I don't mean the kind of time lines used in history classes with dozens of dates. The kind of time line I mean has three main parts: a beginning, middle, and end. Here is how to create one.

- If you are planning fiction, at the top of a page of notebook paper, write the word "beginning." Next to "beginning" write "setting—place and time." Under

Snow Week by a Third Grader

Do you remember the day it snowed in Georgia a few weeks ago? It really happened and I'm going to describe how I enjoyed the day of fun!

#1

First, my brothers and I had a snowball fight in our front yard. Only I made perfectly round snowballs. Zach (my little brother) became my arch nemesis at that fight, so I threw snowballs at his face. He tattled to my mom, but she said nothing.

#2

Secondly, I'm going to tell you about what we did. I was making a snowman. The first snowman I ever built measured 2 feet tall and 1 foot wide. We also used beans for the eyes and mouth, and used a carrot for the nose. Zach told mom about it as soon as we finished.

#3

The most fun thing I did that day was sleigh riding. We used my neighbor's sleigh in his backyard. The sleigh could only fit three people, and I always rode at the back of the sleigh because while we're sliding down, the people who are not on the sleigh threw snowballs at the people that rode the sleigh (mostly at the front person).

#4

After all of that, we went to warm down inside my house to drink some cocoa with marshmallows. We sat near the fire and ate some s'mores and had a wonderful first snow week to play outside.

I wish another snow week will come much later.

Figure 6. The resulting essay from the Figure 4 mind web

"setting" write "characters, opening scene, and problem to be solved." Leave enough space to add the proper details. Use phrases, not sentences.

- If you are planning nonfiction, you might label the beginning, middle and ending differently. The labels might be "childhood," "school years," and "adulthood" or "before the war," "during the war," and "after the war" or "foal," "colt," "stallion."

- For a fiction story, after the beginning section, on your timeline write "middle." This is where you write most of the details of your story. Write phrases, not sentences. Or draw cartoons. Write whatever helps you to organize the action of your story.

- A few lines up from the bottom, write the word "end" if the story is fiction. Here write how your story ends and ideas you need to explain.

- For nonfiction, the parts might be about the same size, but for fiction the middle part should be the longest. I recommend three parts to the timeline, "beginning," "middle," and "end." Three is enough.

Easy? You bet. Does it work? Yes, if there is enough detail. Make sure you have about ten or more ideas in the beginning and middle parts. What follows, Figure 7, is a timeline. From it came the essay in Figure 8.

Babe Ruth timeline by a fifth grader

Intro	one time when Babe pointed to the bleachers and hit the ball there	#1
Childhood	born poor 1895 stole apples from fruit stand chewed tobacco snitched drinks of whiskey from bar threw eggs at cars smoked	#2
St. Mary's	when 5 went to school for bad kids studied math, science, LA met Brother Matthas he was like Babe's father greatest person Babe ever met Babe joined St. Mary's baseball club at 6 played on team of 12-year-olds played pitcher and catcher	#3
Baseball	Babe joined the Baltimore Orioles played for the Red sox played for the Yankees also faced bad times	#4
Ending	slugger percentage	#5

Figure 7. Time line organizer by a fifth grader

Babe Ruth by a fifth grader

In a famous World Series, a slugger walked up to bat. With the count 2 **#1** and 2, the slugger pointed two fingers to the bleachers in left-center field. What happened next became a legend when the slugger walloped a moonshot into left-center field. Home Run! Babe Ruth, a legendary slugger for the Red Sox, Yankees, and Braves became a legend. Even though Babe earned that home run, he had rough times in his life.

Babe was born into a big, poor, family in 1895. Before he turned five he **#2** didn't attend school, he stole apples at a fruit stand, he chewed tobacco, and he snatched drinks of whiskey from his father's bar. His friends and Babe even played in the street, and when a car arrived, they chucked eggs at the car. As a kid, Babe once stole a dollar from his dad to buy ice cream for all of his friends. His angry father spanked him when he returned home, but he didn't learn his lesson and repeated it.

When Babe turned five, his father brought him to a school for bad kids **#3** and kept him there, which sounds bad, but it was the best thing for Babe. Babe started school at St. Mary's studying math, science and LA. One day he ran outside for recess and he noticed a teacher slamming a ball for the students. Later, he joined the St. Mary's baseball club. Because he performed so well at the tryouts, when he was eight, he played for the twelve-year-old team. He pitched and caught.

After he finished St. Mary's, he joined the Baltimore Orioles, a minor **#4** league team. Then the team lost money, so Babe was sold to the Red Sox, a major team, and played pitcher. Eventually, Babe was traded to the Yankees. Later, the Red Sox didn't win a series, so they blamed it on Babe Ruth and called this curse "The Curse of the Bambino." Babe arrived at the Yankees with a $20,000 salary for a year and he played outfield instead of pitcher. In the beginning, with the Yankees, he struggled with a lot of strikeouts in two months and broke a bone. Suddenly, he was slamming home runs and earning a lot of hits. In the end of the season, the Yankees qualified for the playoffs, and then went to the World Series, though they lost to the New York Giants. He performed very badly, so after the World Series he promised the mayor of New York that he would hit better next season. And he did.

Today he's ranked number three in hitting homeruns. He hit 714 **#5** homeruns in a career of 20-30- years.

Figure 8. Essay written from the time line organizer.

2.7 Chart organizers

How are Percy Jackson and Harry Potter the same? How are they different? How are you and your sister the same? How are you different?

For essays like these, where one concept needs to be compared (to show similarities) or contrasted (to show differences), a simple chart is easy to create.

A chart organizer is like a table except that it is well organized.

For the chart organizer, draw two vertical lines on notebook paper, creating three columns. Use the first column to list ideas to be compared or contrasted. At the top of the other two columns write the names of what you are contrasting (for example, WWI and WWII). Similarities can be written over the line separating the second two columns.

Charts, like Figure 9, are good for students who like neat organizers.

On the following page, Figure 10 shows how the Figure 9 chart helped a third grader organize and expand an essay topic.

	Grey Reef Shark	Horn Shark
Grey Reef Sharks and Horn Sharks chart organizer by a third grader		
habitat #1	Indian/Pacific water over continental shelves warm water	North America coastal northwest coastal California over continental shelves warm water
prey #2	carnivore reef fish squid shrimp crab	carnivore fish marine invertebrates hard shell mollusks crustaceans star fish
appearance #3	1 meter short head ridges over eyes two dorsal fins large venomous spines brain grey center dark spots	long slender body large fins rounded snout schools out at night

Figure 9. Chart organizer by a third grader

Grey Reef Sharks and Horn Sharks by a third grader

Grey reef sharks and horn sharks differ in many ways.

#1

Horn sharks live in northwest North America in the United States on the coast of California in warm sea beds. Warm Indian and Pacific Oceans in the Middle East to the islands of the deep Pacific provide habitat for the grey reef sharks. Both sharks survive in warm waters and on the continental shelves.

#2

Shrimp, squid, reef fish, and crab are grey reef sharks' main prey. Invertebrates, hard shell mollusks, crustaceans, starfish and sea urchins are horn shark's main prey. These two sharks eat different prey but they are carnivores. Horn sharks are preyed upon by large fish, sharks and humans while grey reef sharks are preyed upon by humans and large sharks.

#3

One meter in length, a short blunt head, ridges over eyes, two dorsal fins, large venomous spines, brown and gray colors and dark spots across the body describe horn sharks. Long slender bodies, large fins, rounded snout, schools (a large group of fish) and nocturnal behavior (active at night) describe grey reef sharks.

These two sharks are very different and a little bit alike.

Figure 10. Essay written from the chart organizer.

2.8 Venn Diagram organizers

A Venn diagram is something like a table and a list combined. It allows you to brainstorm ideas into two or three categories: how ideas are similar and how they are different.

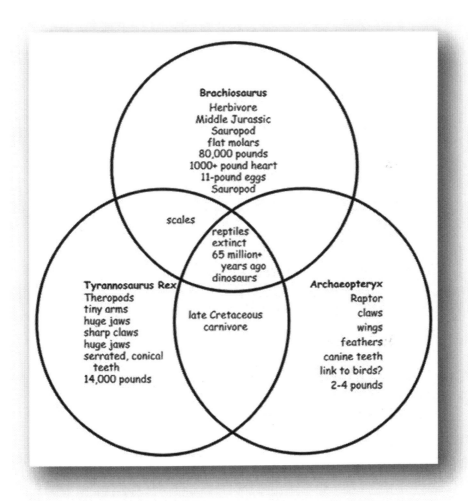

Figure 11. Venn Diagram organizers reveal how ideas are similar and different.

Figure 11 shows a Venn diagram.

Advantages:

- A Venn diagram is easy to make.

- A Venn diagram can be used for up to three subtopics.

Disadvantages:

- A Venn diagram can be tricky if you have three topics.

- After the Venn diagram is complete, it needs to be organized more before you can begin writing.

- Venn diagrams can get messy.

To make a Venn diagram organizer, start with two huge circles that overlap by a third or more. Make sure your circles start out big and overlap a whole lot. Try tracing a seven or eight-inch bowl whose shape fills about two-thirds of a page of notebook paper. If you trace the bowl twice, the part in the middle will be big. That's what you want. In the outer parts of the circles you will list how each idea is different, and in the middle, you will list how they are similar.

If you like mind webs and don't mind a mess, use Venn diagrams. But if you like things neat and clean, use table organizers.

2.9 Formal outline organizers

The most difficult prewriting organizer is the formal outline. A formal outline has both advantages and disadvantages.

Advantages:

- A formal outline uses brief phrases or words, not sentences, except for the topic sentences.

- A formal outline breaks down a topic into clearly identified sections and subsections.

- A formal outline is organized from the first word, so you don't have to do that later.

- A formal outline shows the structure of your essay easily.

- Off-topic ideas or ideas that are not logically presented are easy to spot.

Disadvantages:

- Writing a formal outline goes slowly.

- Writing a formal outline can frustrate you if you think the outline requires you to be too precise.

- Some fifth graders aren't ready for a formal outline and skip using a prewriting organizer because this kind of organizer is so hard.

A formal outline has all the information that a list has, but the information is organized in a precise way. You know what information is to be written in each paragraph and in each sentence. It will take you longer to create a formal outline, but once it's done, it's done. You are ready to turn the information into sentences.

Topic: 3 kinds of dinosaurs
I.   Introduction ending with topic sentence
II. Brachiosaurus
     A. Physical features:
          1. Long neck
          2. Thousand-pound heart
          3. Huge, heavy legs for support
          4. Eggs up to 11 pounds
     B. Diet
          1. Herbivore
          2. Low lying shrubs
          3. Tree leaves
     C. General facts
          1. Sauropod
          2. an earlier dinosaur
III. Tyrannosaurus Rex
     A. Physical features
          1. claws for holding and tearing prey
          2. sharp teeth for ripping prey
     B. Diet
          1. Carnivore
          2. Ate other dinosaurs
     C. General facts
          1. Theropod
          2. a later dinosaur
IV. Archaeopteryx
     A. Physical features
          1. feathers
          2. wings
          3. size of a pigeon
     B. Diet
          1. Carnivore
          2. Ate smaller creatures, eggs
     C. General facts
          1. Raptor
          2. May be the link between dinosaurs and birds
V.   Conclusion: Three favorite dinosaurs, extinction

Figure 12. A formal outline is a precise way to organize ideas for an essay.

2.10 Picture organizers

Sometimes pictures make great prewriting organizers. Suppose you want to explain the life cycle of a butterfly. You might be able to draw the pictures faster than you can write the words. See figure 13.

Or are you just learning how to speak in English? You might not be ready for mind webs, timelines, comparison/contrast charts or Venn diagrams. But you might be able to draw your stories or ideas.

Figure 13. Drawing pictures can sometimes organize ideas faster than putting them into words.

2.11 Why use an organizer?

Organizing your thoughts before you write is one of the best ways to improve your writing.

Yet I see students who create great organizers and then don't look at the organizers when they write. Big mistake. Here's why referring to your organizer leads to better writing:

- You don't have to go back later to move big chunks of text around.

- You can shorten the time you revise by sticking to your plan.

- Instead of focusing on organization as you write your first draft, you can focus on style. You have already thought through the details, so now you can focus on how to present them.

Do you need to use everything in your organizer? If you have included a dozen or more details for each body paragraph, you can skip some of the less important details. But if your number of ideas is skimpy, you need every detail and more.

3.0 Introductions

3.1 Writing introductions is hard.

Writing an introduction is hard for some kids. You might stare at that empty notebook page for ten or twenty minutes. Then, you might write, "Hi. My name is Sid. I'm going to tell you about my pet dog." Or you might write a question like "Do you want to know about my pet dog?"

If this happens, ask an adult for ideas. Your mother might say, "Daisy just had a litter of puppies. Two of them are black, one is brown and one is spotted. Sissy named the spotted one Spot, but we are still thinking about what to name the others." Or your big brother might say, "Spot is such a dumb name for a dog, but that is what Sissy called one of our new puppies. I wanted to call the puppy 'Blob' but Mom said no."

If you like one of the adult's suggestions, write it down your own way. Don't ask the adult to write it down or you won't learn how to write introductions. The adult's job is to get you thinking. Your job is to write the introduction.

Beginning an essay, even if you've written a detailed prewriting organizer, can be hard. But when you have written many essays, introductions become easier.

3.2 Dumb beginnings

Suppose you write, "Hi. My name is Sid. I'm going to tell you about my pet dog." After you write that, you read it and think, "That's lame." What should you do?

Figure 14. Beginning an essay, even if you've written a detailed prewriting organizer, can be hard.

Keep going. That dumb beginning got you started. Dumb beginnings are crutches that get you going when you can't begin any other way. As long as a beginning gets you going, it's not so dumb after all.

After you finish your essay, go back and cross out, "Hi. My name is Sid. I'm going to tell you about my dog." Start your essay with what comes next.

Many crutches begin with "Hi. My name is . . ." But some crutches are questions like "Do you want to know about. . .?"

Is your question interesting? If not, change the question into a more interesting one.

What are some dumb beginnings?

- I am going to tell you about my dog.

- Do you want to hear about my dog?

- Do you have a dog? I do.

- I have a dog. Her name is Bailey. She is a female dog.

- Dogs are so cute.

What are some better beginnings?

- My dog, Bailey, gets so excited when it's time for a walk that sometimes she pees on the floor.

- I've begged for a dog for eleven years, and last week my parents said yes. Finally!

- When you look at all those hopeful caged eyes at the animal center, how do you decide which dog to love?

- Do you know what a mother dog does right after her puppies are born? She licks them, that's what. Yuck.

- Do you think having five kids at a time is normal? Well, it is for my dog."

3.3 How to write a hook

What if, after finding a good topic and organizing it with lots of details, you still don't know how to begin? What should you do?

Write a list of hooks.

For example, suppose you need to write a book report on a novel. Here are some hooks.

- Do you think *Harry Potter and the Sorcerer's Stone* is a good book? I do. (duh)

- What's your favorite novel? Mine is *The Sorcerer's Stone*. (duh)

- I just finished *The Sorcerer's Stone*, and let me tell you, I'm glad I did. (So what?)

- Have you ever raced through a book that you couldn't put down? Have you even read it under the covers with a flashlight? (okay)

- Has this ever happened to you? You are racing through a really good book when you realize that soon the book will end. So, you slow down to make the story last as long as possible. (better)

What usually happens when you write a list of hooks is that you write boring hooks first. But that's okay because writing those boring hooks warms up your brain. Then you write better hooks until you write a really good one you can use.

3.4 Types of hooks

Essay introductions need hooks. But too often, the hooks kids write wouldn't snare a minnow. What kinds of hooks work? Let's take the topic, "When I lost a tooth," and look at some hooks that would make your reader want to continue reading.

Anecdote: (a story from the news, from history, from your family, or from your personal experience)

My Grandpa says he doesn't remember when his first tooth fell out, but he remembers when his last one did. It was after he cracked a walnut with his teeth, and a tooth broke apart. He had to go to Dr. Taylor's office to have that tooth pulled out. Grandpa says that was the most expensive walnut he ever ate.

Analogy/comparison: (This introduction hooks better if the two items being compared seem unrelated.)

A tooth is like a baby's diaper. We don't think much about either of them when they are working fine. But if they are falling out or falling off, that's all we can think of!

Dialog:

Hey, Mom, how much did the tooth fairy bring you?"
"A nickel a tooth."
"A nickel a tooth! That's all?"
"That's all."
"Didn't they invent quarters back then?"

Irony/humor:

Every six or seven-year-old kid loses teeth. Why, there must be millions of kids all over the world right now who can't eat corn on the cob.

Statistics:

When I was in first grade, every single kid lost a tooth, and most of us lost more than one. Billy Ellingham was the champion though. He lost seven teeth that year. I remember because we kept track with a bar graph on the bulletin board.

Startling claim:

Suppose you brush your teeth for a minute in the morning and a minute in the evening every day this year. That's 730 minutes or more than 12 hours standing in front of a sink brushing and spitting.

Compelling question:

Do you know that when a shark's tooth falls out, the shark can grow a new tooth as many times as it needs to?

Generalization:

My Grandma calls my teeth my pearly whites.

4.0 First drafts

4.1 Skip lines or double space

Since writing improves the most when you revise, you need to leave room on your paper for revising.

- **Write on every other line of notebook paper.** Or double space if you are writing on a computer or tablet. That space between lines gives you room to make changes later. Print tiny X's in the left margin of every other line to remind you to skip lines. See figure 15 on the next page.

- **Write on one side of the paper only.** This way, as you start a new page, you can look back at the last few sentences without flipping the paper. Rereading as you write is important. Also, by placing your new blank page just under words you wrote, you don't look at an empty piece of paper. You keep going.

- **Leave one-inch margins on each side of notebook paper** and on the computer.

- **Write darkly** so you can easily read your writing. Use dark blue or black ink, not other colors. You will use other colors later to revise.

- **Use clear handwriting.** Or, if you are using a computer, use an easy-to-read typeface.

Figure 15. Writing improves the most when you revise, so leave room on your paper for revising.

4.2 Write on computers or electronic equipment

If you can compose your essays on a computer or a tablet, you should. Electronic equipment has many advantages.

- You can erase and rewrite easily, so you'll be willing to make changes.

- You can cut and paste easily, moving sentences around.

- You know right away if a word is misspelled, and with one click, you know how to correct it.

- You know if you have a grammar problem.

- You can read what you are writing. Reading your own handwriting can be difficult.

- You are more likely to revise because you can see what you are doing.

- Writing on electronic equipment goes faster than handwriting does.

- Your work looks professional.

4.3 Flow

To write first drafts, good writers seek time when they are unaware of their surroundings, when their minds are living in the writing. This is called "flow."

A quiet background helps. That could mean complete silence or a recording of ocean waves or bird sounds. You need to be able to hear the words in your mind, and sometimes you need to hear the words aloud. Libraries can be good places to write first drafts; so can picnic tables in the back yard.

A noisy background can also lead to flow. But it must be certain kinds of noises, boring low noises. A vacuum cleaner or hair dryer turned on in another room—just left on, with no one using it—can help you to focus. So can the noise machines babies use to fall asleep.

Even people talking can lead to flow if the people are not shouting and you are not interested in what they say. See figure 16 on the next page.

For writing a first draft, flow can be important. For revising, flow can be important too, but it is usually less important. For editing, flow is usually not important.

Figure 16. When writing a first draft, you need to experience flow, a time during which you're able to block out background noise and hear the words you are writing in your mind.

4.4 Transitions

What do you notice about following paragraph?

> First, sedimentary rocks were formed when sediment sifted down under water. Next, more sediment covered the earlier sediment and put pressure on it. Also, the amount of water on top of the sediment increased. Additionally, its weight put even more pressure on the sediment. Consequently, over millions of years, the sediment became rock. Finally,

the rock was thrust up so that we can see its layers today in places like the Grand Canyon.

Every sentence in the paragraph begins with a transition word. Putting a transition word at the beginning of each sentence is not a good idea. It fills your writing with needless, distracting words.

Instead, use words which fit naturally into your writing as transitions. Repeat an important word from an earlier sentence or use a pronoun to refer to a word or idea.

Good transitions organize ideas to keep your reader following clearly, but your reader doesn't notice them.

4.5 How to improve transitions

- Don't start every sentence with a transition word. If you must use transition words that are not part of the writing itself, tuck them into sentences. If you use beginning sentence transitions, cut out half of them; then cut out half of the rest.

- Don't use transition words that contain many syllables. "And," "but," "so," and "since" do the job just as well as "additionally," "however," "therefore," and "because." In general, the more syllables a transition word has, the more noticeable it is.

- Repeat words or use pronouns to refer to words or ideas already mentioned. Those repeated words or pronouns are natural transitions.

Notice how the paragraph about rocks sounds using organic transitions.

Sedimentary rocks were formed when sediment sifted down under water. As more sediment covered the earlier sediment, it increased the pressure. The amount of water on top of the sediment increased and its weight put even more pressure on the sediment. Over millions of years, the sediment became rock. Some of that rock was thrust up so that we can see its layers today in places like the Grand Canyon.

5.0 Conclusions

5.1 Full circle conclusions

The introduction and the conclusion are usually the two most difficult parts of the essay to write. You are like a pilot who finds the take-off and landing the most work, while the middle of the flight is much easier.

When it is time to write your conclusion, reread your introduction. The introduction and conclusion should support one another. "Going full circle" is a common idea in writing—starting with one main idea, developing many subtopics, and returning to the main idea at the end.

Here are some ways to do that, using the "when I lost a tooth" topic. If you can include humor in your conclusion, and leave your reader with a smile, that is usually the best ending possible.

Anecdote introduction:

My Grandpa says he doesn't remember when his first tooth fell out, but he remembers when his last one did. It was after he cracked a walnut with his teeth, and a tooth broke apart. He had to go to Dr. Taylor's office to have that tooth pulled out. Grandpa says that was the most expensive walnut he ever ate.

Anecdote conclusion:

Grandpa says I should bite into a walnut with my wiggly tooth. And I'm tempted after seeing Grandpa's teeth in a glass on his nightstand. What if I lost all my teeth and not just the wiggly one? Imagine all the money the tooth fairy would bring me!

Dialog introduction:

"Mom, how much did the tooth fairy bring you?
"A nickel a tooth."
"A nickel a tooth! That's all?"
"That's all."
"Didn't they invent quarters back then?"

Dialog conclusion:

My mother got a nickel, my older cousin got a dime, and my big sister got a quarter.
"Mom, what's the chance of me getting a half dollar for my loose tooth?"
"Pretty good, honey."
Sometimes it's great to be the youngest.

Statistics introduction:

When I was in first grade, every single kid lost a tooth, and most of us lost more than one. Billy Ellingham was the champion though. He lost seven teeth that year. I remember because we kept track with a bar graph on the bulletin board.

Statistics conclusion:

Now that I'm in fifth grade, no one is losing their teeth any more. But some kids are sprouting. Maybe I could get my teacher to post a bar graph of the number of inches we grow this year. With my dad being six feet two inches, I have a chance of winning that contest!

Startling claim introduction:

Suppose you brush your teeth for a minute in the morning and a minute in the evening every day this year. That's 730 minutes, or more than 12 hours, standing in front of a sink brushing your teeth.

Startling claim conclusion:

Twelve hours brushing teeth in one year times 80 years is about 960 hours in a lifetime. That's 40 days of our lives spent brushing our teeth. Yikes! I better buy a strong toothbrush.

5.2 Looking to the future conclusions

In addition to going "full circle," another good kind of conclusion is one which focuses on the future of your topic.

Suppose you are writing about what you want to be when you grow up, and you write about three or four different careers. In your conclusion you could say that you don't know what your future holds, but you believe it will have something to do with math since all your career choices need a strong background in math.

Or suppose you are writing about different kinds of stars. You could end by mentioning future research or discoveries to be made in the field of astronomy, or a recent discovery and how exciting that is for you.

If you are reviewing changes in statewide exams, you could

conclude that current changes will not be the end of the changes. You could suggest that future tests might be taken on smart phones or tablets.

Introductions	Looking to the future Conclusions
I like the *Artemis Fowl* series better than *Harry Potter* because *Artemis Fowl* has more action than most *Harry Potter* novels.	Even though *Artemis Fowl* contains lots of action, my father says those books will seem lame once I read Dan Brown novels. Library, here I come!
On my first Halloween I had a lot of fun.	Already I can't wait until next Halloween because my past Halloweens have been great!
Last year I went for an eye exam and the doctor said, "Soon you might need glasses."	I can't wait to go to school and see what my classmates will say.

Figure 17. The future conclusion is one which focuses on the future of your topic.

5.3 Asking for action conclusions

If you have written a persuasive or argumentative essay, your conclusion should include a request for action by your reader.

Ask yourself, "Who is my audience?" If the answer is other fifth graders, then think about what actions your classmates could take to do what your essay suggests needs doing. Could they draft a petition and invite classmates to sign it? Could they write letters? Could they ask a community leader to visit the class? Could they hold a work day?

Sometimes you try to persuade your readers to change their ways of thinking. You could suggest your audience read a book, newspaper column or magazine article for more information. You could suggest your audience listen to a podcast or to regularly read a certain blog.

If you are recommending that your classmates exercise more, you could suggest your audience sign up for a sport. Anything that makes the change you suggest easy for your readers is more likely to be tried. So, end your essay with suggestions which are easy to follow.

5.4 Narrative endings

One way to end a story is to look to the future. When J.K. Rolling ended her final Harry Potter book, she leapt forward 20 years to show Harry's, Ron's and Hermione's kids heading off to Hogwarts. This ending takes us full circle, back to Harry Potter's beginning, but not to the same beginning.

Even if your story is a few pages long, you could look to the future. A character could wake up hours after the action ends and remember what happened earlier—with a smile or with a groan.

Another way to end a narrative is to leave the reader with an important emotion. Maybe a babysitter has worked hard to care for a cranky toddler. The babysitter leaves, exhausted. As she looks back, she sees the toddler smiling and waving.

Another way to end is with action. Superman stories end with Superman solving a problem and flying off to solve another problem. He flies off because that is an easy way for the writer to end one story and make you, the reader, want the next one.

If you use dialog in your narrative, then ending with dialog or the thoughts of a character makes sense. Use dialog to create a mood, the last impression which you want the reader to have.

Do you need to explain everything at the end? No. If the details are not important, let the reader guess at them. That's part of the fun for the reader.

6.0 Revising

6.1 Read your essay aloud

When we read with our eyes, we find some mistakes. But when we read aloud and use only the words on the page, we hear other mistakes.

- Is something missing—a word, a word ending, a sentence? Is a whole idea missing? Add it now.

- Is a word or an idea duplicated? You might write the word "the" at the end of a line and then write the word "the" at the beginning of the next line.

- Are ideas out of order? You can number whole paragraphs to rearrange them. You can circle sentences and mark them with arrows to move them. You can even cut up your essay and paste it back together again in a different order.

- Is a connection unclear? Sometimes the reason you say something is clear in your mind, but the reader might not understand. Make sure you have connected ideas, so the reader isn't confused.

- Are ideas incomplete? Complete them.

- Every subtopic sentence should support the main idea of the essay. Check to see that each one does. If a sentence doesn't belong, cross it out so you can stick to one main idea.

- Are words overused? If words like "then," "just," "so," "really," "like," and "because" are overused, eliminate most of them.

6.2 Replace weak verbs

The next step in revising is to identify verbs and to replace weak verbs with strong specific verbs.

With a colored pencil or highlighter, mark each main verb and each verbal. You can ignore helping verbs. On a separate paper make a list of those verbs, using tally marks to show how many times you use each verb. Present, past, and future—all forms of a verb are treated as the same verb. So are all forms of irregular verbs such as "is," "are," "was," "were," "be," and "been." They are the same verb, the verb "to be."

If you don't know what a verb is, ask an adult to check your essay to be sure you find all the verbs. It's easy to overlook linking verbs, but they need to be counted.

Look at your list of verbs with their tally marks. What do you notice? You might say, Well, I used an awful lot of "get" and "got" and also "is" and "are." You should notice if you use some verbs often.

How often is too often? In a typical piece of student writing, three or more uses of the same verb is too many. But there are exceptions.

Some verbs haven't many synonyms. "Play" is such a verb. How do you say, "I play the piano" or "I play soccer" without using the word "play"? "Read" has almost no synonyms.

When a verb is part of an idiom, it can be hard to replace.

am, is, are, was, were	have, has, had	get, got	go, went
come, came	make, made	take, took	say, said
do, does, did	think, thought	tell, told	show, showed
put	leave, left	know, knew	see, saw

Figure 18. Overused verbs to replace.

6.3 How to replace weak verbs

Replacing weak verbs with strong, specific verbs leads to good writing. How do you do that?

After you identify weak or overused verbs, start with easy words to replace, such as "get," "go," "do," "make," and "take." Read aloud the sentence in your essay using a weak verb and think of a more specific word.

In the sentence, "I go to JFK Elementary School," for example, you might think about the word "go." "I study in" or "I attend" would be better than "I go." Cross out the word "go" and write "study in" or "attend" in the space above the crossed-out word. Then move on to the next word.

Use a dictionary or a thesaurus. For the sentence, "I gave the dog a bath," you need to know that a verb is always listed in the present tense, so the word to look up is "give," not "gave." Notice that "give" has many meanings. You need to choose a meaning that works for your sentence. Not every synonym for a word works in every sentence.

Part of an essay with verbs revised by a rising sixth grade student.

sat rose
...we ~~were~~ on regular seats on a theater stage. Then, the curtains ~~went up~~.
scanned spotted
My eyes ~~looked at~~ the whole room and ~~saw~~ my parents. I could hear the
trembled
clapping and the screaming of babies. My heart ~~beat~~ in fear as my palms
sweated shook One hundred eighty students gathered for
~~got wet~~. My legs ~~trembled~~. ~~There were 180 students graduating.~~ First,
graduation. participated in the principal distributed
our school honored the people who ~~did~~ clubs. Second, ~~they gave out~~
received smiled,
presidential awards for best academic grades. When I ~~got~~ one I ~~was full~~
looking at my parents. accepted
~~of joy and happiness~~. Third, we ~~got~~ our diplomas from our teachers...

Figure 19. An example of revising overused verbs

Rarely can you replace every weak verb. That is okay. Replacing many of them will improve your writing. See Figure 19 for an example of revised verbs.

6.4 How to replace "to be"

The hardest verb to replace is the verb "to be'" in its many forms: "am," "is," "are," "was," "were," "been," "be" and "being." This verb is probably the one you use the most.

The problem is that "to be" hardly ever has strong synonyms. It can sometimes be replaced with another linking verb. "She is sick" can become "She looks sick" or "She feels sick." But those changes don't improve your writing.

Even harder is when the verb identifies something that exists. How do you restate, "That dog is mine"? Let me know if you find out.

Usually you need to replace not just the verb, but the whole sentence. First, ask yourself what you are trying to say. For the sentence, "She is sick," how do you know she is sick? What does she look like that would let you know she is sick? You might say, "Her face is red, and she has a fever." That's good, but you are still using the word "is." How can you say the same idea without using the word "is"?

How about, "Her mother placed an ice bag on her flushed forehead." Or, "'Wow! 101 degrees,' said her mother shaking the thermometer." Or, "The child lay down on the cold tile floor, moving her flushed body every few seconds."

The trick is to let your reader hear, touch, smell, taste or see (usually see) what you saw in your mind before you wrote, "She is sick." "She is sick" is a conclusion based on certain evidence. What is the evidence? Those facts are what the reader needs to know to conclude that "she is sick."

Figure 20 on the next page is part of a third grader's revised essay which replaces "is" and "are."

Colossal squid, ~~are~~ one of the

biggest animals in the world,

~~They~~ live in the bottom of the

Antarctic waters where ~~there is~~
       reaches. These
no sunlight^. ~~Colossal~^
cold-blooded
^ squid ~~are cold-blooded and~~
move very slowly.

Figure 20. The hardest verb to replace is the verb "to be'" in its many forms.

6.5 Use active verbs

What are active verbs? In a sentence with an active verb, the subject does the verb. For example,

- "The cat licked her paw." The cat (the subject) did the licking.

- "Lee ate a sandwich." Lee (the subject) did the eating.

What are passive verbs? In a sentence with a passive verb, the subject does not do the verb. In fact, we may not know who does the verb.

- "I was followed home by a dirty dog." I (the subject) does not do the following.

- "Homework was assigned today." Homework (the subject) did not do the assigning.

What are the advantages of active verbs?

- Active verbs make your writing easy to understand.

- Using active verbs is a more concise way to write.

- Your writing zips along with active verbs.

Then, why do we have passive verbs?

- Passive verbs can hide the doer of an action. Sometimes we don't want to say who did the action, or we might not know who did the action. "The last cookie had been taken."

- Passive verbs can confuse. Sometimes a writer wants to keep the reader confused or in suspense. "The man was watched as he stepped out of his car. As the man leaned over, he was noticed by a toddler in a carriage,"

- Passive verbs can slow down action.

Most of the time, it's better to use active verbs.

6.6 Replace weak words

Relying on the same overused words makes your writing dull, so it's good to replace them. Replacing as you write your first draft is the best way, but you can return later and replace overused words or phrases, such as:

- **There is, there are, there was, and there were.** When you start a sentence with "there," you are moving the subject after the verb, weakening the subject. And since the verbs "is," "are," "was," and "were" are weak verbs to begin with, you doubly weaken the sentence. Instead, rewrite the sentence, starting with the word which comes after "there is." For example, "There is my grandmother. She bakes every day." Change to "My grandmother bakes every day."

- **Very.** You might think that by putting "very" in front of an adjective you strengthen that adjective, as in "her very cold hand." In fact, "her cold hand" is stronger. If you absolutely, positively think you need "very," then find a different word to express what it means. "Her icy cold hand" shows coldness better. Or write a simile. "Her hand, cold as a dead fish," conveys temperature and adds creepiness.

- **Stuff.** "Stuff" is a word you use when you are too lazy to think up a specific word. "I packed my suitcase with some stuff." What stuff? Money? Ballet tutus? Dirty socks? Say what you mean. The reader cannot read your mind.

- **Thing, anything, something, and everything.** Like "stuff," these words tell the reader you are lazy. Use a specific word.

- **Just.** "Just" is a filler word, a word that allows you to think longer about what you want to say next. If you write "just" in front of a verb, go back and cross it out. Like "very," "just" is rarely needed.

- **So, then, like.** Many kids start sentences with these words or use them after the word "and." Almost always the writing is better if you take "so," "then," and "like" out.

- **Etc.** "Etc." means "and more." Tell your reader what the more is.

Exception:

- When you are writing dialog, you want the dialog to sound real. Kids say "stuff," "then" and "like," so use the words people say in dialog, even if those words are weak. You want your characters to sound real.

6.7 Avoid using "-ly" adverbs

Adverbs are parts of speech which describe verbs, adjectives, adverbs and whole clauses. Most adverbs end in "-ly," such as "quickly" and "awfully." (But not every "-ly" word is an adverb.) The "-ly" adverbs are considered weak words by many writers because they tell, not show. For example,

- Weak: The toddler walked quietly to bed.

- Stronger: The toddler tiptoed to bed.

- Weak: That baby is tired.

- Stronger: That baby yawned.

- Weak: The awfully pretty child looked at us flirtatiously.

- Stronger: The beautiful child smiled at us.

We need some adverbs. We don't have negative versions of most verbs, so we use the adverb "not." "Yesterday," "today," and "tomorrow" provide crucial time information, as does "now" and "then." When we are organizing an essay, sometimes it makes good sense to use "first," "next," and "finally."

As a rule, try not to use adverbs which end in "-ly." Instead, strengthen your verbs.

6.8 Vary sentence beginnings

Here is the way many children write:

> Today I woke up and ate breakfast. Then I got on the school bus with my friend, Olivia. I sat near the window. I put my backpack on a hook at school and I sat down. I did my morning work first, and then I said the pledge. I did math until it was time to go to specials.

Do you notice that almost every sentence begins with "I," and the two sentences that begin with another word use "I" as the second word? How does this sound? Boring.

Here's how to improve the beginnings of sentences. Identify the first word of every sentence (not every line) by highlighting it or encircling it with a colored pencil. You want the first words to stand out.

Read the highlighted words aloud and listen for repeats. When you hear them, ask yourself if you can replace the repeating word with another word. A noun can be replaced with a pronoun. A proper noun can be replaced with a common noun.

If a prepositional phrase is used at the end of a sentence, can it be moved to the beginning of the sentence?

An adverb can be added to the front of a sentence. But don't do this often or it will sound added on.

Sentences can be combined to eliminate repeating first words. Suppose you write, "I did my morning work. I did math. Then I went to specials." These little sentences can be replaced with "I did my morning work, did math and went to specials."

Figure 21 on the next page shows how a third grader changed some first words of sentences.

6.9 Vary parts of speech at sentence beginnings

If you can identify the parts of speech that you use to begin sentences, you can vary them to improve your style. Here is how.

After you have circled the first word of each sentence, identify each word's part of speech. Make a list of the parts of speech and use tally marks to identify how many times you use each type. You will probably notice that you rely on the same parts of speech to open sentences. You will also notice that you don't use certain parts of speech. See Figure 22 on the next page.

Seismosaurus or earthquake lizard

had a super long neck and body. ~~Its~~
The   for this animal was
^total body length ^ ~~is~~ one-hundred

and thirty feet long and fifty feet

tall. It weighed eighty thousand
                    and was
pounds. ~~It's~~ ^ the third largest
          When Seismosaurus walked,
dinosaur ever to live. ^
     its   which measured
~~Its~~ ^ neck ^ ~~was~~ one half of its body,
~~and its neck~~ moved from side to side.

Figure 21. By varying sentence beginnings, you make your writing more interesting.

Next, go back over the essay and look at the overused parts of speech and try to vary the openings by using underused parts of speech.

- Do you use prepositional phrases to start sentences? Many kids use prepositional phrases only later in sentences.   Move a prepositional phrase to the beginning.

- Adverbs and conjunctions are often overused as first words, especially the words "so," "also," and "then." Eliminate most of these words to start sentences.

- Verbs are rarely used as sentence openers because when you start a sentence with a verb, you ask a

---

Out of 20 sentences in a student's essay, the following analysis of sentence openers shows frequent use of adverbs and articles, but verbs, subordinate conjunctions, gerunds and infinitives were not used at all. Knowing this, a student can improve his writing style by including the other parts of speech as sentence openings.

nouns I	phrases I
pronouns II	coordinate
articles IIIII	conjunctions III
adjectives I	subordinate
verbs	conjunctions
adverbs IIIII II	gerunds
prepositional	infinitives

Figure 22. To improve writing style, open sentences with different parts of speech.

question. Yet asking a question varies the sentence type from a declarative to an interrogative. Plus, a rhetorical question—a question which you answer in a moment—can seem elegant.

- Most kids don't put the dependent clause of a complex sentence at the beginning of a sentence. Changing the order of parts of a sentence can change the opening. "I arrived late to school after my alarm didn't ring" becomes "After my alarm didn't ring, I arrived late to school."

6.10 Use dialog

Do you ever turn the page of a book and see long paragraphs? And then far down the next page you see a section of dialog? What do you do? Do you skip the long paragraphs? Do you beeline to the dialog?

Dialog makes writing sparkle. One reason *Junie B* books are so popular is that Junie B and her friends speak in dialog on almost every page.

Sometimes when I read a student's writing, I suggest, "This would be a good place for dialog." The student might have people talking anyway, but the student uses indirect speech, such as "Eve said that she has homework." Compare that to, "'I have homework,' said Eve."

Dialog can also be a great hook in the introduction of an essay, if the person speaking says something worth hearing. Compare "Honey, breakfast is ready" to "Honey, a heaping plate of blueberry pancakes is calling your name."

One warning: When you learn the power of dialog, you might want to write only dialog, leaving out setting and nonverbal action. If you do, your writing will be confusing.

Figure 23 on the next page shows how a first grader writes dialog.

6.11 Use "said"

Using specific vocabulary words leads to good writing, but there is one exception, the word "said."

"Told," "stated," "remarked," "revealed," "whispered," "shouted," "spoke"—the list of substitutes for "said" is practically endless. But most of the time, "said" is best.

When you write, "She said," you are saying that a person spoke, but you are not telling how she spoke. In the sentence, "Jack said, 'I am soaking wet from that rain,'" the focus is on what Jack said aloud, as it should be. In the sentence, "Jack hollered, 'I am soaking wet from that rain,'" the focus is split. Part of the focus is on what words Jack said aloud, and part is on his manner of speech—a holler.

You are so used to reading the word "said" that it almost disappears, much like the word "a." That's good. You need to know who is speaking, but usually how they speak is not important. By using any word other than "said," attention goes away from what is said to how it is said, which you usually don't want.

A good rule is to use "said" if you want your reader to focus on the words which were said aloud. However, if you want

Notice how a first grader handled dialog and setting.

In chapter three of <u>Cam Jansen and The First Day of School Mystery</u>, Cam Jansen and Eric were meeting their new fifth grade teacher, Ms. Benson. When they got there, two police officers walked in the classroom.

They asked Ms. Benson, "Did you drive your green car to school this morning?"

Ms. Benson said, "Yes."

One of the policemen said, "You left the scene of an accident."

Ms. Benson quickly said, "No I didn't. There must be some mistake."

"Please follow us," said one of the police officers. Then they took her away.

After they took her away, Danny jumped out of his seat and said, "My mother said don't get in trouble. Well, I didn't. My teacher did. She got arrested."

Figure 23. Dialog makes writing sparkle.

your reader to focus on the way someone speaks, then use another word. But rarely do that.

Compare these two versions of the same conversation:

"I'm hungry," Joyce stated.
"Well, what do you want?" asked Joyce's mother.
"I want a donut," demanded Joyce.
"Well, you can't have one," her mother replied.
"You're mean," Joyce responded.
"Part of the job," Joyce's mother answered.
"What does that mean?" asked Joyce.
"It means no donut," Joyce's mother retorted.

"I'm hungry," said Joyce.
"Well, what do you want?" said Joyce's mother.
"I want a donut."
"Well, you can't have one."
"You're mean," said Joyce.
"Part of the job."
"What does that mean?"
"It means no donut," said Joyce's mother.

Did you notice that in the first version of the conversation, you were thinking about two things: what was said and how it was said? In the second version, you were focusing mainly on what was said. And in the second version, because not every line of conversation identifies the speaker, the conversation goes faster and sounds natural.

Use said unless your teacher tells you to use synonyms.

6.12 Mix S, CP, CX and CP/CX sentences

Most writers use declarative sentences. Those declarative sentences are four types: simple, compound, complex and compound-complex. Good writers use all four types, but they use complicated simple sentences and complex sentences more.

Once in a while, look at the sentences in one of your essays and identify them by type to know what kinds you use and don't use.

- If you have many simple sentences, you might be writing (and thinking) too simply. Small, uncomplicated sentences are mostly simple sentences. But if you have an abundance of clear yet complicated simple sentences, you are writing well.

- What is a complicated simple sentence? It might start with a prepositional phrase. It might add a compound subject or predicate and include a direct object or predicate adjective. It might delight with details such as appositives and adjectives. The kinds of complicated simple sentences are endless.

- If you have many complex sentences, your writing might be too complicated, especially if the average number of words per sentence is more than 20. A high mix of complicated simple sentences and short complex sentences, with a few short simple sentences thrown in, almost like spices in a recipe, usually results in attractive writing.

- You might write complex sentences well but nearly always begin those sentences with independent clauses. If you turn some of those sentences around—starting with the dependent clause—you will add sentence variety without much effort.

- To find out if you overuse compound sentences, circle all the "and," "but," and "so" words which connect clauses. Now write the same ideas without using "and," "but," or "so." You will create more imaginative sentence structures.

- Compound-complex sentences generally are long. Using many of them makes your writing difficult to read. If yours are long, cut them into two or three shorter sentences.

A **simple sentence** contains one complete subject and one complete predicate, or one complete subject and more than one complete predicate; or more than one complete subject and one complete predicate.

A **compound sentence** is two or more simple sentences joined by a coordinate conjunction (and, but, or, nor, so, for, and yet) or by a semicolon.

A **complex sentence** contains one independent simple sentence (a clause) joined to one or more dependent simple sentences (clauses) by a subordinate conjunction or by certain pronouns.

A **compound-complex sentence** contains one or more complex sentences joined by a coordinate conjunction or semicolon to a simple sentence.

6.13 Increase the number of words per sentence

Little children write tiny sentences. Their writing sounds childish because each short sentence contains one idea. (I have a dog. His name is Rex. Rex barks.) By writing longer sentences, you improve your writing. (My dog, Rex, barks at other dogs.)

Tiny sentences are almost always simple sentences. Kids think that if they add a conjunction, their writing improves. Usually, it doesn't. (I have a dog and his name is Rex and Rex barks.) You need to form longer sentences without relying on "and," "but," and "so."

When you write longer sentences, your sentence grammar becomes more interesting. The grammar goes from short simple sentences and string-along compound sentences to more adult-like sentence structures—complicated simple sentences and complex sentences. This is why you should count words in sentences. The actual number is not crucial but improving the sentence structures is. If you count words, you will probably see that you are writing too many short simple sentences.

You want some long sentences and some short sentences, but you don't want all long sentences or all short sentences.

6.14 Count the number of words in your sentences

Most little kids write fewer than seven or eight words in their sentences. Good older writers write an average of 15 to 20 words per sentence. You probably need to increase the number of words in your sentences.

Begin by counting the number of words in each sentence (not on each line) and record the number in the margin near the sentence. Don't write the number where a sentence ends, or it will be hard for you to find the number later. If you write the number with a colored pencil, you'll find it easier.

Next, add up the total number of words. That means add up all the margin numbers you have written down. Then add up the total number of sentences. That means add up the number of numbers in the margin (easy if the numbers are in colored ink).

Now divide the total number of words by the total number of sentences to find the average number of words per sentence (bigger number divided by smaller number).

You never want your number to average more than 20. If it does, that means too many of your sentences are too long. See Figure 24 on the next page.

If you use interjections like "Wow!" or "Amazing!" you should not count those words as sentences.

If you write dialog, you will write short sentences because people speak in short sentences. Calculate just the sentences without dialog. Don't eliminate dialog to increase the number

First grade writing before revising:

5   4
I went to the store. I bought a lollipop. It was
3   4   4
broken. I took it back. The man said, "Sorry."
5
He gave me another lollipop.

First grade writing after revising:

10
I went to the store where I bought a lollipop.
8
But when I got home, it was broken. When I
15
took it back, the man said, "Sorry," and he gave

me another lollipop.

Figure 24. Revising 4- and 5-word sentences to 8-, 10- and 15-word sentences.

of words per sentence. No! Dialog is more important than a number.

Wait to count words until after you have revised your sentences. Otherwise, you'll have to do it again after you revise.

6.15 How to increase words: Add details

Suppose you want to increase the number of words in your sentences. How can you do that? One way is to add more details to your existing sentences.

Adding details increases the number of words. More importantly, it changes a general, boring essay into a specific, interesting essay. What are details?

Proper nouns. If you mention your school, write its full name. If you mention your home, mention the city and state. If you mention your teacher, name your teacher.

Numbers. How many friends threw snowballs? How many snowballs did you throw? How many minutes did you throw snowballs? Use numbers.

Dates, time of day, or seasons. Make sure you write down these details rather than think them.

Sensory feelings, smells, sounds, and tastes. Try to add the information from all your senses—how cold the snow feels, how fragrant the hot chocolate smells, or how warm the air feels as it leaves your nose.

Size and color. "Blue" can mean many shades of color. Look up synonyms in a thesaurus or write a simile—blue as the sky on a cloudless day.

Getting inside someone's head. Explain what someone is thinking. "My brother hit me with a snowball. So, I threw one back at him." Why did you throw it back? Were you mad at him or were you having fun? Let the reader hear what your characters are thinking.

Adding dialog. Instead of "My brother and I decided to have a snowball fight," how about this: "'Hey, let's see who can hit that tree the most,' my brother said. I said 'Sure,' and began packing snowballs." The information is the same, but with dialog, the reader is emotionally connected.

Feelings. Even though a character might be piloting a space ship over Mars, the reader can identify with the character when you explain her fear or excitement.

Adding examples. If you want to show how much it rained, you can say, "For example, the iris roots were covered with an inch of water." Or "My little cousin says words funny. She says 'dog-EEE' when she sees a dog and 'No, no yuck' when she sees the dog's dish of food."

6.16 Add alliteration, similes and hyperboles

On rubrics, figurative language is included in the section marked "style." What kinds of figurative language are easy to insert?

Alliteration. This means repeating a consonant sound as in "Peter Piper picked a peck of pickled peppers." Two words beginning with the same consonant sound are usually enough, and those words don't need to be right next to each other either.

To write alliteration, find a noun beginning with a consonant. Now think of an adjective or prepositional phrase that begins with the same letter as the noun, such as a "large linden tree" or a "chocolate bar with a chewy center." If you are writing fiction, change names. John F. Kennedy School can become John Jefferson School. Or add to a name to provide alliteration. Mary can become Mary Margaret.

Similes. Similes are comparisons using "like" (my cat is like a tiger) or "as. . .as" (my cat is as fierce as a tiger). Similes are better if they have some connection to what you are writing about.

For example, you could describe sticky buns "as sticky as a stamp on an envelope." Both are sticky, but the buns are a food and the stamp is a paper. Instead, identify another delicious food that is sticky. "My sticky buns are as sticky as peanut butter on my teeth" provides a closer comparison.

Hyperbole. Hyperbole is the extreme exaggeration of an idea. "I ate a whole pizza last night" might be hyperbole, but "I ate every pizza in the grocery store" is clearly hyperbole. "I had five hours of homework last night" might not be hyperbole, but "I have enough homework to last me until I am 70 years old" is hyperbole.

Usually when kids write hyperbole, they don't exaggerate enough. Think about what is possible but unlikely (not hyperbole) and what is clearly impossible (hyperbole).

When you write figures of speech, you should also consider the tone of your writing. Hyperbole works well in humorous writing, but it sometimes changes the mood of a more serious piece. If your writing is serious, use another form of figurative speech.

6.17 Add metaphors and allusions

Metaphors and allusions can be hard to use, but they also make your writing sound more sophisticated than alliteration, similes and hyperbole.

Metaphors are comparisons which don't use "like" or "as." To write metaphors, start by using "is" and say something is something else, especially if the something else seems odd or far-fetched. For example, "My cat is a mouse exterminator," or "My dog is my alarm clock" are metaphors.

Next, try leaving out "is. "My dog, Buster, my alarm clock, wakes me for the school bus."

Metaphors usually require more practice than similes, but they are more powerful comparisons, capable of bringing adult style to your writing.

Allusions are references to myths, stories, people, works of art, books, movies, the Bible, Shakespeare's plays and anything else which your reader recognizes. Choose a reference which your readers will understand without your explaining it. Harry Potter, Percy Jackson or Goldilocks can be used. So can Bart Simpson if you think your readers will know who he is.

For example, if you are writing about an annoyed mother who is telling her son to come out of his room, the mother could say, "You better come out or I'll huff, and I'll puff, and I'll blow your door down." Notice that in this example, the big, bad wolf from the Three Little Pigs is alluded to but not named. Or in describing a big sister, you could write, "She has the looks of Sleeping Beauty and the brains of Hermione

Granger." You assume your readers will know what you mean by Sleeping Beauty and Hermione Granger.

Even if every reader doesn't recognize your allusions, you should use them. J. K. Rowling uses allusions when naming some of the characters in the *Harry Potter* books. For example, by naming Professor Snape with a name that sounds so much like "snake," she makes us fear him.

Figure 25. A mountain of books is a metaphor.

6.18 How to increase words: Combine sentences

Combining two or more sentences usually causes the number of words per sentence to rise slightly. But more importantly, you improve the structure of your sentences.

To combine sentences, look for short sentences. Usually, but not always, two short sentences need to be next to each other to combine them. Always they need to be in the same paragraph.

When you find a short sentence, see if the short sentence can be combined with the one before or after it. They need to be close in topic or show relationship—a cause and effect, a sequence, or dialog by the same person, for example. They need to be the same type sentence: declarative, interrogative, exclamatory or imperative. If the sentences

Here are revisions by a sixth grade that combine
sentences about a swim meet.

I raced in heat 3 of the girls 11-12 200-yard medley
                    Even though   **to swim**
relay for backstroke. I was supposed ~~to do~~

breaststroke, I was forced to do backstroke because

the swimmer went on vacation. The girl I replaced is
             I am   . **When griped to**
better than ~~me~~ by 2 seconds, so I ~~told~~ my mom.' I asked

her to call the coach and say I dislocated my arm,

skinned my nose and broke my toe. "No," she said.

Figure 26. A sixth grader improved her writing by
combining short sentences into longer sentences.

seem related, think about how they can be combined without
forming a compound sentence.

Keep in mind what sounds normal for you to write. If you are
a second grader or an ELL student, choose words you know.
If you are a fifth grader or a more widely read student, try
using some new vocabulary words. Look for synonyms in a
thesaurus. "Sometimes my little sister asks a silly question.
I say a silly answer and she laughs at me." How can these
eight and ten-word sentences be combined? You might add
the word "when" after the word "sometimes." "Sometimes,
when my little sister asks a silly question, I say a silly answer
and she laughs at me." You have gone from a simple sentence

and a compound sentence to a compound-complex sentence. Your new sentence is 19 words, but the sentence sounds normal for a fifth grader.

How about this example? "First, snowball fighting. We had the fight in our front yard. I was the one who made perfectly round snowballs." The third-grader who wrote this fragment and two tiny sentences changed them to "First, my brothers and I had a snowball fight in our front yard where I made perfectly round snowballs."

6.19 How to increase words: Eliminate sentences

When a sentence contains almost no new information, you should eliminate it and put its tiny bit of information into another nearby sentence.

For example, suppose you write, "My little sister's name is Mackenzie. Mackenzie is three. She is curious." The second sentence has only one new bit of information, Mackenzie's age. The third sentence has only one new bit of information, that Mackenzie is curious. The second and third sentences can be eliminated, and their information can be put into the first sentence. "My three-year-old sister, Mackenzie, is curious."

What kinds of sentences are good ones to eliminate?

- A sentence that begins the same way as the previous sentence.

- Sentences containing one idea.

- Sentences which repeat information but say it slightly differently. Choose the clearer version.

6.20. Identify the range

The range is the number of words in the sentence with the largest number of words minus the number of words in the sentence with the smallest number of words.

Why is knowing this number useful?

If the range is in the single digits, this means most of your sentences are about the same length. Your writing seems boring.

If the range is in the high teens or low twenties, you have written some longer sentences and some shorter sentences. Readers find this kind of writing interesting.

If the range is in the high twenties or thirties, this means your writing might be hard to understand. But if only one sentence is long, then your writing might not be hard to follow.

You probably need to increase the range of your writing. To do that, you need to be aware of sentence range and force yourself to write sentences of varying lengths.

Notice the following introduction to an essay written by a fifth grader:

> Have you ever played Monopoly? If you have, then you know all about it. If you have not, then let me describe Monopoly to you.

The first sentence has 5 words, the second sentence has 9 words, and the third sentence has 11 words. 11 minus 5 equals a range of 6. If the rest of the sentences in this essay are about 5 to 10 words long, the range would be small, and the essay would be boring.

Compare that to the beginning of a narrative written by a rising second grader:

> Once when I woke up I found a baby unicorn in my tiny bed. It looked as tall as me with a tail and wings, a purple and pink horn, and a white and yellow body. Right away I jumped on the unicorn and flew to a castle that is made of glass. She said I owned the castle.

The first sentence has 14 words; the second has 22 words; the third has 17 words; and the fourth has 6 words. 22 minus 6 equals a range of 16, an excellent range for such a young writer. Notice also that all three sentences vary in length by 4 words or more. The writing about a unicorn is more interesting than the writing about Monopoly.

By combining sentences or adding more detail, you usually bump up the number of words per sentence. But don't eliminate all short sentences. That is a mistake. Including short sentences is essential to good writing.

Did you notice in the last paragraph that a 17-word sentence was followed by a 6-word and a 4-word sentence? A really short sentence after a long sentence adds style.

6.21 A well revised draft looks a mess

If your revised first draft shows cross outs, arrows, circles, and erasures, that means you have truly improved your essay. See Figure 27.

Every professional writer knows that the real work of writing happens when you revise. If you think you have revised your essay, and your draft looks about the same as when you started, you have probably not revised enough.

On the other hand, if your draft has cross-outs, arrows, words squeezed in, circles to identify verbs and first words of sentences, and perhaps even sections cut apart and taped together in a different order, plus numbers in the margins, you have revised.

Revising is not editing. Revising means making big changes in your writing to improve it. Editing means making small changes.

Your parents might be shocked if they see your writing while you are revising it. If this happens to you, show them examples of your drafts and the final versions of those drafts. Let them see that you will correct the tiny errors eventually. Usually this suffices.

6.22 What about perfectionists?

Do you insist on starting over if you forget to skip a line or if an erasure leaves a smudge? If so, I encourage you to tolerate messy first drafts because, when you revise well, the writing will become messy.

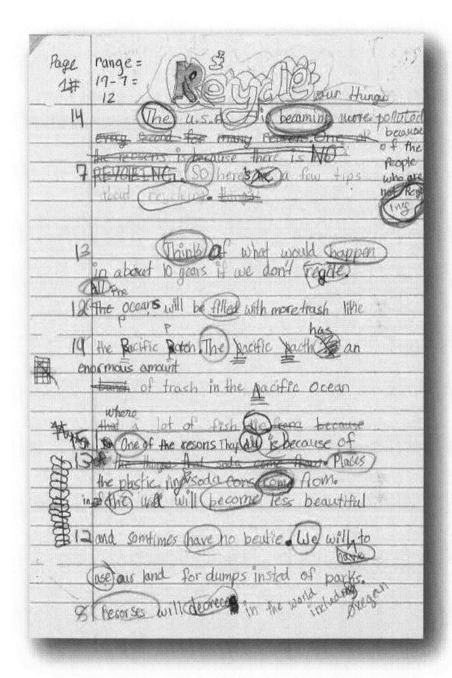

Figure 27. Here is an example of a fourth grader's messy but revised essay.

If you are a perfectionist, you might never revise unless you learn to tolerate some mess. I worked with one student who needed to start over so many times that she never completed a single essay. But I have worked with other perfectionists who learned that the mess increases their chances of higher grades.

7.0 Editing

7.1 How to find errors

Computer software programs will find many of your spelling and grammar errors, but not all. Some common errors are

- **Spelling**. Check for spelling and meaning of "there," "their," and "they're"; "its" and "it's"; "to," "too," and "two"; "an" and "and"; and "then" and "than."

- **Apostrophes**. Check to see if the apostrophe is in the right spot and if the word really needs an apostrophe.

- **Subject/verb agreement**. If you have words between the subject and the verb, it's easy to match the verb with the wrong word.

- **Third person singular present tense**. These verbs usually have an "s" or "es" at the end of the word. Irregular verbs such as "has," "does," and "goes" are needed as helping verbs for some tenses.

- **Run-ons and fragments**. All sentences must have a subject and a predicate.

- **Quotation marks**. Check to see if every quotation has both beginning and ending quotation marks. If someone is talking, often you need a comma after the word "said."

- **Paragraphs**. In English, all writing is done in paragraphs. If you hand write, you need to indent. If you type, you can indent or not, but if you don't, you need extra spacing between the paragraphs to visually show the start of a new paragraph.

- **Articles**. Do you mix up "an" with "and"? Do you forget to put "an" before a word which begins with a vowel sound? Check.

- **Then**. Then is not a conjunction. If you use it like a conjunction, be sure to add "and" before the word "then."

Here's a trick which can help you find errors. Read your essay backwards. Read the last sentence first. Next, read the second last sentence. Then, read the third last sentence. Reading sentences out of order helps you see mistakes. Even better: read the sentences out of order out loud so you can both see and hear the mistakes.

7.2 Print your essays

Rarely do you see your own writing printed unless you type it yourself. But the effort is worth it. You can look at your final draft with pride. That is the moment when you realize you are a writer.

On the next four pages is a sixth grader's essay which has gone through all the stages: prewriting organizer in the form of a time line, revised essay, and final typed draft.

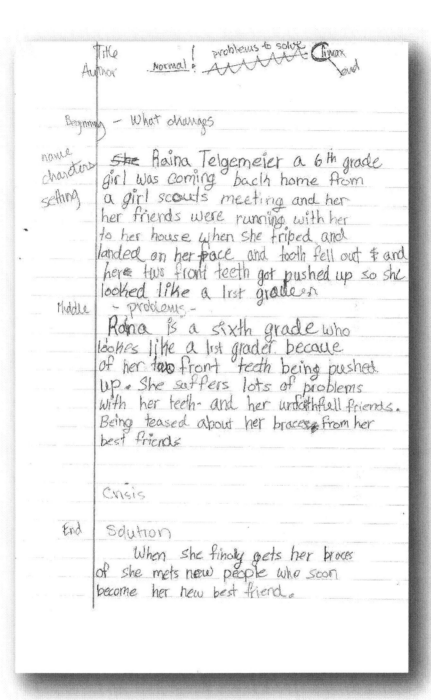

Figure 28. A fifth grader's time line prewriting organizer

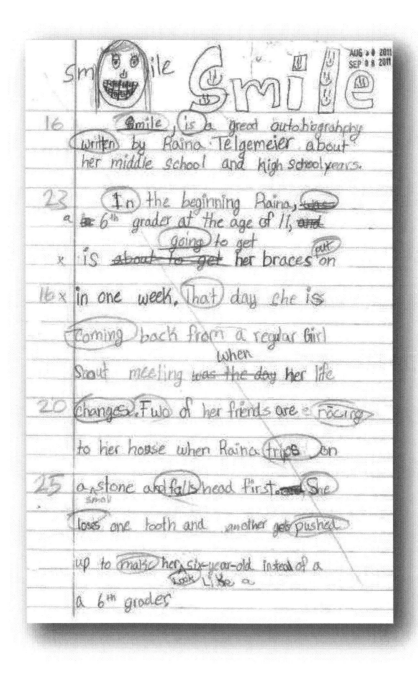

Figure 29. The first page of the two-page handwritten revised draft.

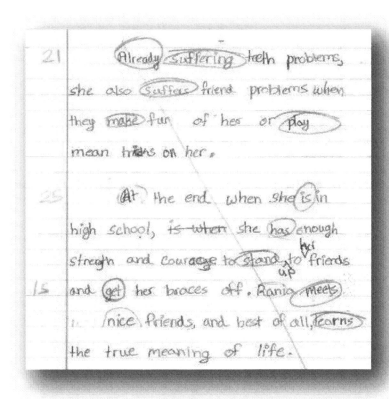

Figure 30. The second page of the two-page handwritten revised draft.

"Smile" by a Fifth Grader

"Smile" is a great autobiography written by Raina Telgemeier about her middle school and high school years.

In the beginning Raina, a 6th grader at the age of 11, is going to get her braces put on in one week. That day she is coming back from a regular Girl Scout meeting when her life changes. Two of her friends are racing to her house when Raina trips on a small stone and falls head first. She loses one tooth and another gets pushed up to make her look like a six-year-old instead of a 6th grader.

Already suffering teeth problems, she also suffers friend problems when they make fun of her or play mean tricks on her.

At the end when she is in high school, she has enough strength and courage to stand up to her friends and get her braces off. Raina meets nice friends and best of all, learns the true meaning of life.

Figure 31. The final typed essay

8.0 Publishing

8.1 How to publish

Professional writers write for an audience. It may be a few people—a neighborhood blog—or it might be more people—newspaper articles. For you to do your best—for you to want to produce the best writing possible—publishing is essential.

How can you publish your writing?

- Hang a finished essay on the refrigerator.

- Photocopy the finished essay and mail it to Grandma.

Figure 32. When you write to be published, you are motivated to write better.

- Scan the finished essay into the computer and email it to aunts and uncles or former teachers.

- Use the finished essay as Mom's screen saver.

- Put a finished copy in a three-ring binder on your coffee table or in your classroom for other students and parents to read.

- Put the finished essay online in a student blog or teacher's blog.

- Put your essay online in a "great essays" section of a teacher's classroom work.

- Enter your writing in writing contests.

Publishing matters. Professional writers write to be read. Most students don't have this opportunity. But when you do, you write better.

At my home, I have a binder of student essays which students read. They want to know what other students have written. Sometimes they then write about the same topic or in the same style as an essay in the binder. I point this out to students whose work has inspired other students, and they grin ear to ear.

Parents, too, read the writings in my binder. They read to enjoy their own children's writing and for the sheer pleasure of enjoying good writing.

9.0 Appendix

9.1 Fifth Grade Writing Standards as specified by the Common Core Standards

The Common Core Initiatives have listed what kids should learn in each grade in each subject. These ideas are broad, but they can be more narrowly defined by state education departments. The ideas are also narrow enough to serve as the state guidelines.

Here are the Standards for fifth grade writing. (For more information on other grades or other subjects, go to http://www.corestandards.org/ELA-Literacy/.

I. Text Types and Purposes

W.5.1. Write opinion pieces on topics or texts, supporting a point of view with reasons and information.

- Introduce a topic or text clearly, state an opinion, and create an organizational structure in which ideas are logically grouped to support the writer's purpose.

- Provide logically ordered reasons that are supported by facts and details.

- Link opinion and reasons using words, phrases, and clauses (e.g., consequently, specifically).

- Provide a concluding statement or section related to the opinion presented.

W.5.2. Write informative/explanatory texts to examine a topic and convey ideas and information clearly.

- Introduce a topic clearly, provide a general observation and focus, and group related information logically; include formatting (e.g., headings), illustrations, and multimedia when useful to aiding comprehension.

- Develop the topic with facts, definitions, concrete details, quotations, or other information and examples related to the topic.

- Link ideas within and across categories of information using words, phrases, and clauses (e.g., in contrast, especially).

- Use precise language and domain-specific vocabulary to inform about or explain the topic.

- Provide a concluding statement or section related to the information or explanation presented.

W.5.3. Write narratives to develop real or imagined experiences or events using effective technique, descriptive details, and clear event sequences.

- Orient the reader by establishing a situation and introducing a narrator and/or characters; organize an event sequence that unfolds naturally.

- Use narrative techniques, such as dialogue, description, and pacing, to develop experiences and events or show the responses of characters to situations.

- Use a variety of transitional words, phrases, and clauses to manage the sequence of events.

- Use concrete words and phrases and sensory details to convey experiences and events precisely.

- Provide a conclusion that follows from the narrated experiences or events.

II. Production and Distribution of Writing

W.5.4. Produce clear and coherent writing in which the development and organization are appropriate to task, purpose, and audience. (Grade-specific expectations for writing types are defined in standards 1-3 above.)

W.5.5. With guidance and support from peers and adults, develop and strengthen writing as needed by planning, revising, editing, rewriting, or trying a new approach.

W.5.6. With some guidance and support from adults, use technology, including the Internet, to produce and publish writing as well as to interact and collaborate with others; demonstrate sufficient command of keyboarding skills to type a minimum of two pages in a single sitting.

III. Research to Build and Present Knowledge

W.5.7. Conduct short research projects that use several sources to build knowledge through investigation of different aspects of a topic.

W.5.8. Recall relevant information from experiences or gather relevant information from print and digital sources; summarize or paraphrase information in notes and finished work and provide a list of sources.

W.5.9. Draw evidence from literary or informational texts to support analysis, reflection, and research.

- Apply grade 5 Reading standards to literature (e.g., "Compare and contrast two or more characters, settings, or events in a story or a drama, drawing on specific details in the text [e.g., how characters interact]").

- Apply grade 5 Reading standards to informational texts (e.g., "Explain how an author uses reasons and evidence to support particular points in a text, identifying which reasons and evidence support which point[s]").

IV. Range of Writing

W.5.10. Write routinely over extended time frames (time for research, reflection, and revision) and shorter time frames (a single sitting or a day or two) for a range of discipline-specific tasks, purposes, and audiences.

Index

Figures

Made in the USA
Las Vegas, NV
23 November 2020